1 $\frac{50}{}$

Girard Essays

THE QUALITY OF LIFE

James Michener

1970

AN URBAN PLANET?

Barbara Ward

1971

PAUL NADLER WRITES ABOUT BANKING

Paul Nadler

1972

THE NEW MAJORITY

Patrick Buchanan

1973

The President and the Author

THE
NEW
MAJORITY

President Nixon at Mid-passage

by Patrick J. Buchanan

"Without the generous opportunity for which I
thank Girard Bank, this book would not have
been possible. But the interpretations,
the views, the words, are all my own; and for
the contents, I alone take full responsibility."

Written for and published by Girard Bank · February 1973

Patrick J. Buchanan is Special Consultant to the President and is widely recognized as the conservative voice within the White House. His duties have included overseeing the preparation of the President's daily news summary, the gathering of background materials and briefing papers for presidential press conferences and assistance in the drafting of presidential speeches and statements.

Mr. Buchanan joined Mr. Nixon as Executive Assistant in January of 1966 and, upon Mr. Nixon's election, became a member of the President's immediate staff. A distinguished writer and nationally recognized authority on the Nixon Administration, Mr. Buchanan is the author of numerous articles that have appeared in the nation's press. He is a former reporter, financial writer, and editorial writer for the St. Louis *Globe-Democrat*.

Mr. Buchanan is an honors graduate of Georgetown University, the Graduate School of Journalism at Columbia University and is a member of The President's Commission on White House Fellows.

Ollie Atkins is the personal photographer to President Nixon and Chief White House Photographer. He has been a member of President Nixon's Staff since 1968.

"The New Majority" is printed on recycled paper.
Copyright 1973 by The Girard Company
Library of Congress Catalog Number 73-77-083.
Printed in the United States of America.

IN LATE DECEMBER OF 1972, just prior to the Christmas holidays, there appeared at my office door two gentlemen to discuss the preparation of an essay about the Nixon administration. It was agreed that Buchanan should write, and the Girard Bank would publish, the former's personal reflections on the past, present and future matters of concern to both the Nixon administration and the nation.

This book was to be the fourth in a series, undertaken by Girard, as a public service. Accompanying the offer was the promise of complete freedom of expression for the author.

The promise was honored; the Christmas and New Year's holidays set aside; and this slim volume is the result.

Without the generous opportunity for which I thank the Girard Bank, it would not have been possible.

But the interpretations, the views, the words, are all my own; and for the contents, I alone take full responsibility.

Patrick J. Buchanan

Patrick J. Buchanan
Special Consultant to the President

January 31, 1973

It has been the purpose and intent of the Girard essays to provide a forum for inquiry and discussion of significant issues of our times. Each year a subject of major importance has been selected and a learned author commissioned to articulate a viewpoint, with the guarantee of complete freedom of thought and expression.

We asked our first author, James A. Michener, to define and discuss major social challenges of the day. His essay "The Quality of Life" was widely acclaimed as a distinguished discourse on problems of the city, race, education, youth, communications, environment.

The mounting plight of our cities prompted us to commission Barbara Ward, worldwide authority on urban affairs, to write our second essay. Her book "An Urban Planet?" proposed a strategy for achieving decent, manageable cities.

Growing concern with national and international financial crises suggested an essay on banking and finance as the third in our series. Dr. Paul Nadler, nationally recognized financial expert, wrote his essay "Paul Nadler Writes About Banking" as his interpretation of the financial aspects of our economy.

This year it seemed important to seek better understanding of the philosophy, policies and programs of President Nixon as his administration entered upon a second term. After careful study, we asked Patrick J. Buchanan, Special Consultant to the President, a member of his staff since 1966 and an authority on the Nixon Administration, to write this year's essay with complete freedom to select subjects that he believed to be the most meaningful and comment freely upon them. We hope "The New Majority" will give readers a useful analysis of the Nixon years as interpreted by a long-time associate of the President.

"The Quality of Life", "An Urban Planet?" and
"Paul Nadler Writes About Banking" are out of print.

Contents

President Eisenhower, Vice President Nixon,
David Eisenhower, Julie Nixon

Campaigning in the New Hampshire Primary (February 1968)

Triumph and Tragedy

*"Mr. Nixon has had vast political experience;
he is a man of obvious competence and capacity;
but unless a political miracle occurs,
he is not likely to compete for important
electoral public office ever again."*
— New York Times
November 8, 1962

A S THE LIMOUSINE carried the President and President-elect down Pennsylvania Avenue to the Capitol, 20 January 1969, Richard Nixon could look back on 1968 as a year of immense personal triumph. Defeated for the Presidency by John F. Kennedy in the closest election of the century in 1960, he had two years later sought the Governorship of California and lost by 300,000 votes.

His career in apparent ruins, he delivered to the press critics of 16 years what *Newsweek* called the "most extraordinary farewell in modern political history." In a biting valedictory to public life, immortalized in political lore as the "Last Press Conference," he declared: "You won't have Nixon to kick around any more because, gentlemen, this is my last press conference."*

*At his arrival in New Hampshire to enter the nation's first presidential primary, February 1, 1968, Mr. Nixon and aides toyed with, but rejected, the idea of opening the campaign kick-off press conference with a line suggested by Wall Street Journal columnist, Alan Otten, "Gentlemen, it looks like you're going to have Nixon to kick around again."

Within a week one network carried a half-hour documentary, "The Political Obituary of Richard M. Nixon." Convicted perjurer Alger Hiss was among those called upon to say a few words over the grave.

While Nixon supporters were aghast at network taste and ethics in dredging up Hiss to evaluate the career of the former Vice President, they could not disagree with the verdict: That career was over.

Concurring himself, Mr. Nixon pulled up his California stakes and moved to New York to begin a new career as a Wall Street lawyer.

Six years after the Long March from California to New York, he had conducted a primary campaign that has become a political classic, reunited his reconstructed party, won nomination on the first ballot, and captured the White House in what critics conceded was perhaps the greatest comeback in the nation's political history.

At Christmas of the same year, he stood beside his younger daughter, Julie, as she married the only grandson of patron and predecessor, Dwight Eisenhower.

Truly for Richard Nixon 1968 was a year of personal triumph. But that same year that had brought him his personal triumph brought also great tragedy to the nation. Not since the depression had America experienced such a crisis of confidence as gripped her in 1968. Not only in anticipation and hope for the future, but in agony and disillusionment with the past, America had turned in November to new leadership.

Yet 1968, which had brought America so much sorrow, had opened on a note of cautious hope.

During the previous summer, the supremacy of

Israeli arms had extinguished in six days a war that threatened to involve the Great Powers, and the June summit between the American President and Soviet Premier at Glassboro, New Jersey, persuaded the nation that another crisis had passed. The fires of Newark and Detroit had been banked and the troops withdrawn. General Westmoreland had come home in November to tell Congress and country the effort in Southeast Asia was on the threshold of success.

Before January of 1968 was over, optimism had vanished. On the 25th of the month, during the Lunar New Year Truce in Vietnam, the armies and political cadres of the Viet Cong rose in the countryside and marched on the cities.

The Tet Offensive—which history may one day rank among the decisive battles of the twentieth century—was underway.

After weeks of fighting which saw enemy troops occupy the old capital of Hue, and besiege the American Embassy in the modern capital of Saigon, 50,000 Viet Cong lay dead. The enemy had suffered the greatest single military defeat of the war, but in the United States he had scored a stunning psychological victory, for the scale and fury of the attack had broken the confidence of many Americans in a successful outcome to the war.

Five weeks later, on March 12, President Johnson, a write-in candidate, was triumphant in the nation's first presidential primary in New Hampshire. His victory, however, was buried beneath the headlines and reams of copy on the astonishing 42% of the vote amassed by his defeated opponent, Senator Eugene McCarthy.

Within a week of McCarthy's moral victory,

Senator Robert F. Kennedy announced for the nomination. On March 31, two weeks later, and two days before the second primary in Wisconsin, President Johnson announced a partial bombing halt of North Vietnam, and his intention not to seek again the office he had won in 1964 in one of the great landslides in U.S. history.

Four days after Johnson's thunderclap, the nation was horrified when Dr. Martin Luther King, Jr., pre-eminent leader of the civil rights movement, was shot down on a motel balcony by an ex-convict in Memphis, Tennessee.

Within hours, King was a martyr and dozens of American cities were paralyzed by rioting and looting. From Washington, D.C., where the worst of the disorders occurred, the world was treated to photographs of smoke pouring over the United States Capitol and the White House defended by Federal troops with automatic weapons.

On the political front, while the nation's press focused upon the hotly contested Democratic primaries, Mr. Nixon . . . whose first opponent, Governor Romney, had retired from the primaries, and whose second, Governor Rockefeller, had declined an invitation to enter . . . continued his uninterrupted march through New Hampshire, Wisconsin, Indiana, Nebraska, Oregon and South Dakota, amassing record votes along the way.

On May 28, 1968, Richard Nixon claimed the greatest primary triumph of his career, garnering some 70% of the vote in the three-way Oregon contest against well-financed campaigns on behalf of Governors Reagan of California and Rockefeller of New York. The same night, in the same hotel,

Robert F. Kennedy was conceding the first defeat suffered by a Kennedy, and pledging to redeem it a week later in California.

On June 5, ten minutes after claiming that victory, Robert Kennedy lay mortally wounded in the kitchen of his Los Angeles headquarters hotel, the second Kennedy in half a decade to fall victim to an assassin.

In August, Richard Nixon and Hubert Humphrey, two war horses dating to the mid-forties, were nominated by their respective conventions on the first ballot. But where the Republican gathering at Miami Beach was marked by the customary hoopla, the Democratic Convention in Chicago featured bitter recriminations within the convention hall and violence in the streets, as harassed and badgered police charged and clubbed a rag-tag army of dissidents and demonstrators who had come to Chicago to vent before the television cameras their contempt for Humphrey, Daley and LBJ.

While America was transfixed by events in Chicago, the world was stunned by the headlines from Czechoslovakia. As the Spirit of Geneva had expired in Budapest, the Spirit of Camp David at the aborted Paris Summit, so the Spirit of Glassboro was dying in Prague at age 14 months.

"What guarantees can you give us that the old days will not return?" the young of Czechoslovakia had demanded of Alexander Dubcek. "You; you, the young people of Czechoslovakia, are that guarantee," Dubcek had responded.

But, in Eastern Europe in the twentieth century, idealism and the spirit of freedom are regular victims of the big battalions, and Soviet paratroops and armor crushed the Prague Spring in an exercise as militarily impressive as it was morally appalling.

Arriving at the Capitol that January morning in 1969, the President was aware of the state of the nation and the ambiguity of his mandate.

In the 57% of the popular vote that had gone against Hubert Humphrey, the bitter fruits of liberalism at home and gradualism in Vietnam had been rejected. But if clear what Americans had voted *against,* what specifically had they voted *for?*

The President's margin of victory was less than one percent; his total percentage, the smallest of any victorious candidate in half a century; his vote in victory 3 million fewer than his vote in defeat eight years before. And, for the first time since the era of Millard Fillmore and Zachary Taylor, his countrymen had seen fit to install a newly elected first-term President—with both Houses of the Congress in the grip of the opposition.

But more than control of Capitol Hill rested with men unsympathetic to the revived political fortunes of Richard Nixon. The sixties . . . an era that had ushered in inflation, an unprecedented wave of crime, ghetto riots, disorders on dozens of campuses, and an endless, winless war in Southeast Asia consuming 300 American lives a week . . . was the Silver Age of political liberalism. This was the era when liberals dominated not only the political but the intellectual and cultural life of the nation. Their party controlled Congress, the White House and the bureaucracy. Their philosophy was in bloom on the Warren Court. Almost without exception, the preeminent niches in journalism and communications, in the academic world and the Big Foundations, in publishing and the arts, were occupied by liberals. Though the November election had given the White House to the man who led their list of least admired Americans, still, their positions of preeminence in other American institutions remained secure. And they were neither without the resources nor the disposition to make life unbearable for their old antagonist now occupying the Oval Office as heir to Franklin Roosevelt and John F. Kennedy.

Aware that the Liberal Establishment was unreconciled to the political verdict of 1968, cognizant of the narrowness of his mandate, Mr. Nixon's first political act, as President-elect, was to extend the olive branch to the vanquished.

His victory pledge to "bring us together," his Inaugural call for Americans to "go forward together," were models of reconciliation and restraint. His White House staff was structured to reflect the nation's political diversity with Goldwater conservatives in uneasy harness with Ripon liberals, and Rockefeller Republicans like Henry Kissinger entering the Presidential service alongside Kennedy Democrats like Daniel Moynihan.

To achieve a truce, an armistice with his adversaries, the President in effect offered more: To forego the victor's prerogative of purging the Democratic bureaucracy and to renew the lease on most of the Great Society programs dear to their hearts. In exchange, he sought a decent interval to initiate and carry out his plan to end with honor American involvement in the Vietnam war.

Eight months into his Presidency, the unwritten understanding collapsed.

Speaker of the House John McCormack, President Nixon,
former President Lyndon B. Johnson

'A Trauma of Distasteful Reversal'

*"It is becoming more obvious with every
passing day that the men and the movement that
broke Lyndon Johnson's authority in 1968
are out to break Richard M. Nixon in 1969.
"The likelihood is great that they
will succeed again."*

— David Broder
Washington Post
October 7, 1969

IF IN THE SUMMER OF '69 there were harbingers
of the fall to come, they were difficult to detect. As
the disillusioning decade was ending, America
seemed entering an Era of Good Feeling. Armstrong
and Aldrin had walked upon the face of the moon;
and American prestige soared. When they returned
to the Pacific, the President was there to greet them
on behalf of an elated and grateful nation.

From there the President flew to Guam to an-
nounce a new foreign policy more consistent with
the new global realities, a policy that sought conspicuously to balance American commitments
against American resources. Then, the President
proceeded on around the world. En route, he visited
American troops in the war zone, thousands of
whom, he had publicly announced, would be returning home to the United States. Then, for the first
time, an American President made a state visit to a
Communist capital of Eastern Europe, and the re-

ception in Bucharest, its spontaneity and warmth, exceeded all expectations.

Returning home, the President unveiled his program to reform the nation's archaic and costly welfare system. Notices from every shade of political opinion were enthusiastic. Rarely had a presidential domestic policy been accorded such an ovation.

His most successful month behind him, the President in early August flew off to the Western White House at San Clemente. When he returned to the Capitol after Labor Day, the clouds had gathered and the storm was about to break. The issue: Vietnam.

Supported and encouraged by their ideological allies in Congress, the press and the academic community, skilled young anti-war organizers had planned the largest demonstration in the nation's history to force the President's hand in Southeast Asia. Their media coverage rivaled that of the Normandy Invasion.

David Broder was among the first to perceive and analyze the character of the coming confrontation. On October 7, his widely quoted column, "The Breaking of the President,"—(quoted at the outset of this chapter)—appeared in the *Washington Post.*

One week later, *Newsweek's* banner read, "Nixon in Trouble" and the cover story ran thus:

> *"From almost every quarter last week the nine-month-old Administration of Richard M. Nixon was under sustained and angry fire, and increasingly the target of the attacks was Mr. Nixon himself and his conduct of the Presidency . . ."*

The foreign policy, civil rights and economic initiatives of the President had all gone awry, declared *Newsweek,* and

"Against this background of disarray, drift and ineffectuality, thoughtful men in both parties found themselves beset with serious doubts about the President's essential ability to lead the nation."

Time magazine, which devoted two successive covers to the demonstrations and the war, was even more exasperated. By October 23, they had had just about enough of the President's stubborn refusal to jettison his policy and admit defeat.

"Instead of making pronouncements about not being the first U.S. President to lose a war, instead of faulting the opposition at home for his difficulties in Southeast Asia, Nixon would perform a better service by preparing the country for the trauma of distasteful reversal."

In retrospect, the writer at Time, and the demonstrators about whom he and his colleagues had been waxing eloquent, were the ones who should, at that point, have been bracing themselves for the "trauma of distasteful reversal."

'For the President had determined that his constitutional authority was being challenged by an arrogant and unelected elite, emboldened by a few hundred thousand street auxiliaries; that, therefore, the time had come to take the question of who would make American foreign policy over the heads of his critics to the ultimate bar, the American people.

In the words of Cactus Jack Garner, the time had come "to give it to 'em with the bark on."

Like other crucial addresses of his quarter century career . . . the fund speech in 1952, the acceptance speeches in 1960 and 1968 . . . the November 3rd address was drafted by the President himself.

In setting his thoughts to paper, the President had reached several basic decisions. First, the political truce with the nation's Liberal Establishment had been broken by them, not by him.

Second, since the challenge was not merely over policy, but over principle—over his constitutional authority to construct a foreign policy without being stampeded by street demonstrators—the issue could not be compromised or conceded. The challenge had to be met head-on.

Engaged then in a confrontation he had not sought, aware that only one—he or his critics—could emerge victorious, the President, on November 3, 1969, delivered what he would privately term, "perhaps the most crucial address of my Presidency."

A long speech as Nixonian presidential addresses go, it reviewed the history of the war and the situation the President inherited, underscored the Vietnam commitments of three Presidents, delineated the consequences of the policies the demonstrators were urging, revealed secret peace initiatives the Administration had undertaken, restated presidential determination not to be driven from his course, iterated the new principles that would govern American policy—and called upon the "great silent majority of my fellow Americans" for support.

> "Let us be united for peace. Let us also be united against defeat. Because let us understand, North Vietnam cannot defeat or humiliate the United States. Only Americans can do that."

Public support was overwhelming. Tens of thousands of telegrams and letters poured into the White House; the President's approval rating in the Gallup Survey rose to 68%, the highest before or since. Only 19% of the American people felt the President was not doing a good job.

Not only had the President hurled back the challenge, he had exposed an enormous gap between the beliefs of the average citizen and the views of those who dominate the public dialogue. Despite its virtual monopoly on the creation and dissemination of information, the liberal aristocracy was exposed as out of touch with the common man, politically unprepared for the "trauma of distasteful reversal."

On November 3, 1969, the President had gone to the people to renew his mandate to govern, and they had returned it overwhelmingly. Looking back, at year's end, upon those critical weeks of the Nixon Presidency, Mr. Broder wrote:

> "If one had to identify a crucial moment for the President in his first year, it would be his handling of the October and November anti-war demonstrations. These were, in a fundamental sense, an effort by the intellectual elite to obliterate the 1968 election and take from the President his mandate to govern.
>
> "With few exceptions, the men and women who can claim to be the country's important thinkers lent their names, their counsel and their prestige to the mass demonstrations against his policies in Vietnam.
>
> "But their effort to 'break the President' failed— and its failure has left the protestors more isolated in their opposition than ever before.
>
> "The intellectual community has come out of this battle with deep wounds, and self-doubts that are as serious as they are well-merited."

13

President Nixon addressing the Nation

Mr. Nixon and The Big Media

*"The national media is a melting pot where
the journalists, regardless of background, are
welded into a homogenous ideological mold
joined to the liberal establishment and
alienated from the masses of the country."*
— Robert Novak,
April, 1972

AWAITING THE PRESIDENT'S November
3rd address, the national networks did not dawdle
in anticipation. Two hours before Mr. Nixon—his
Presidency in the balance—took his case to the
country, the NBC and CBS evening news warmed
up their national audiences with atrocity reports,
the latter featuring some particularly horrid film of a
South Vietnamese soldier stabbing an enemy pri-
soner to death.

ABC's contribution was to sign up for post-
speech commentary W. Averell Harriman, architect
of the disastrous Laos agreement of 1962, which all
but ceded the Ho Chi Minh Trail to the military
planners in Hanoi, and chief American negotiator
at Paris who in eight months head-to-head with his
Communist counterparts had won agreement on the
shape of the table.

The reaction of Mr. Harriman, like that of the
network "analysts," to the President's address was
doubt, disappointment and disagreement; they did
little to disguise their hostility.

In the White House there arose the view, uncontradicted by network performance, that in this most critical confrontation, the networks had openly sided with "the men and the movement" seeking to force the President into new concessions.

Thus it was that, ten days later, Vice President Agnew arrived in Des Moines to settle the account.

The purpose of the Vice President's address . . . "the greatest sustained polemic in the English language in the twentieth century" in the estimation of one media analyst . . . was not simply the settling of an account. It was the opening of a national debate upon the power, the responsibility and the fairness of network news.

Protesting their innocence of the Vice President's charges, network newsmen and executives argued that television news simply holds up the mirror to reality, and network newsmen cannot be held accountable for what that mirror reflects. But the analogy of the mirror is less exact than that of the searchlight. Network news does not "mirror" American society.

On the contrary, the television camera, like a powerful searchlight, picks out only tiny fragments of reality, which it magnifies and presents to the nation. Repeated selection of the same kind of fragment can leave the nation with the wholly false impression that the fragment is representative of the whole.

Those who determine what goes before the country nightly as "national news" have the power to present to Americans the picture of a land of peace and prosperity, generosity and tolerance—or, a land of strife and turmoil, poverty and racism.

They can present a Utopian landscape of American society that leaves the nation unprepared for social disruption—or, they can so immerse the public in the negative and seamier sides of American life as to convince millions that ours is assuredly the most wretched society on the face of the earth.

Because only a tiny handful of men in three corporations exercise that enormous power, one cannot readily concur in Mr. Cronkite's disclaimer that he and his colleagues are altogether unaccountable for the consequences of what they convey.

"I don't think it is any of our business what the moral, political, social or economic effect of our reporting is."

Yet, the traumatic effect of reportage from Vietnam caused Mr. Cronkite's own colleague, Roger Mudd, to wonder aloud, "whether in the future a democracy which has uncensored TV in every home will ever be able to fight a war however moral or just."

If television news can so sap a democracy's will as to render it incapable of fighting for its ideals, then the "effect of our reporting" should be a major concern, not only of Mr. Cronkite, but of the people of the United States.

And because networks are the principal source of information for half the nation, the people have a right to know what biases and prejudices inform network judgment in selecting—and rejecting—the "news" that goes nightly into forty million homes.

If we are to believe not only the Vice President, but the testimony of distinguished scholars and journalists such as Howard K. Smith, Robert Novak, Rowland Evans, Irving Kristol, Paul Weaver, Kenneth Crawford, Richard Wilson, Robert Bartley, Arthur Krock, Daniel P. Moynihan, James Keogh, James J. Kilpatrick and Edith Efron—then the particular "biases and prejudices" are those of political "liberalism."

Within the media many will concede readily this bias, and retort, "What else is new?" What is new is not the existence of the liberal bias. What is new, in the last decade, is the wedding of that bias to unprecedented power. Men who are taking an increasingly adversary stance toward the social and political values, mores and traditions of the majority of Americans have also achieved monopoly control of the medium of communication upon which 60% of these Americans depend as the primary source of news and information about their government and society. And these men are using that monopoly position to persuade the nation to share their distrust of and hostility toward the elected government.

The first of these facts explains the diminishing confidence of the American people in the objectivity and fairness of network news. The second partially explains the present state of relations between the networks and the national government.

True, there has always been tension between Presidents and the press; it is a time-honored American tradition. And true, also, that Richard Nixon and the liberal press have been sparring partners for a quarter century. But the growth of network power, and its adversary posture toward the national government, is something beyond that tradition—something new in American life.

The executives, anchormen and correspondents of the network news would have us believe they are the direct descendants and heirs of John Peter Zenger and Elijah Lovejoy. That is not the case.

These men are not victims of society or government in any sense of the word. They are ranking members of the privileged class, the most prestigious, powerful, wealthy, influential journalists in all history. The corporations in whose studios they labor are not struggling journals; they are communications cartels, media conglomerates holding positions within their industry comparable to that of Ford and General Motors.

Not three men in the U.S. Senate enjoy the celebrity status or wield the influence over American opinion of a Cronkite, a Sevareid, a Brinkley. Not even the elected President of the United States enjoys their nightly privilege of untrammeled access for their unchallenged views into twenty million American homes.

To listen to a $150,000-a-year network commentator telling his audience of 20,000,000 that second-echelon government officials are cruelly tramping upon his First Amendment rights is unimpressive.

In counter-attacking against what they view as unwarranted Administration criticism, the networks go to the nation and declare that their fight is the people's fight, that they are only fighting for the "people's right to know."

But, as columnist and political analyst Kevin Phillips wrote with acid pen to that network claim:

"Phooey. What people's right to know what information? Joe Suburbanite's right to know how the Department of Health, Education and Welfare coddles bussing or how the Vietnam mess was originally blueprinted by foundation and Ivy League liberals or how liberal profiteers are making fortunes off subsidized housing, poverty programs and environmental consulting busi-

nesses? Hell, no. You never see that kind of investigation in the liberal media. "The public's right to know" is a code for the Manhattan Adversary Culture's desire to wrap the First Amendment around its attacks on the politicians, government and institutions of Middle America."

The passage seems self-explanatory.

And not only is much of the nation's political leadership, Democrat and Republican, alarmed over the marriage of left-wing bias and network power. So also are many within the academic and media community; and if the polls are to be believed, so also is a majority of the American people. The networks have a serious problem that is the nation's problem as well.

Simply stated it is that an incumbent elite, with an ideological slant unshared by the nation's majority, has acquired absolute control of the most powerful

The President and staff members
H. R. Haldeman, John D. Ehrlichman, Ronald Ziegler

medium of communication known to man. And that elite is using that media monopoly to discredit those with whom it disagrees, and to advance its own ideological objectives—and it is defending that monopoly by beating its several critics over the head with the stick of the First Amendment. But, surely, the perpetuation of such monopolies was not what Mr. Jefferson had in mind when he wrote from Paris urging Mr. Madison to include in the new Constitution a separate Bill of Rights. Rather, it was precisely such arrangements that Mr. Jefferson likely had in mind when he asserted, "In questions of power, then, let us hear no more of trust in men, but rather bind them down from mischief with the chains of the Constitution."

Critics should not be distracted by cries of "repression", and public tears over the "death of the First Amendment." Nothing in our Constitution, written or inherent, prevents individuals in government or private life from devising and proposing ways and means to crack this unprecedented concentration of political power, to open up the national airwaves, to guarantee that a broader range of information and opinion is brought before the American people.

Efforts to insure that the spectrum of opinion on America's airwaves reflects more the diversity of the American people would seem fully consistent with, not hostile to, what this nation has always represented.

Dr. Milton Friedman, distinguished economist and disciple of Adam Smith, believes the long-range answer lies in more and competing channels of communication, to be achieved partly through the rapid expansion of cable television. But that is a long-range solution; and reforms can be made in the short run that can not only help to close the network's credibility gap with the American people, but improve the existing and unhealthy atmosphere.

The first would be recognition by the networks of the special responsibilities inherent in a monopoly situation—namely, to guarantee "balance" in commentary. CBS, with its introduction of the "Spectrum", an editorial series in which individuals of a broad range of views are heard, has recognized the principle. The practice could easily be introduced into prime time.

Secondly, while many network commentators and correspondents claim to be the people's "representatives" in Washington, the claim is suspect.

True "representatives" of the people can be fired or re-hired by the people at regular intervals—election time. To whom do the gentlemen of the networks answer, other than some nameless executive, whose principal concern is less the welfare of the nation, than the Nielson ratings and profit margins. As Herman Kahn observes, contrary to media claims, there is no element in American life more out of touch with the concerns and beliefs of the common man than the liberal press. The Washington-New York journalistic establishment is no more the "people's representative" than is Common Cause the "People's Lobby."

To bring the networks back into closer touch with the American people, a conscious search might be made for newsmen and anchormen and commentators around the nation who feel and share the views and beliefs and the will to investigate and report and comment on the issues that most concern the American people—and not simply those of greatest interest to its Liberal Establishment.

Third, while no crime for a Washington journalist to oppose or abhor or detest the incumbent Administration, the assignment of such a newsman to be the principal conduit of information about that Administration to twenty million Americans every day seems a prima facie case of bias. The assignment of network reporters remains the network's decision, alone. But the journalistic desire for objectivity would seem to dictate that one not assign Herbert Marcuse to cover the New York Stock Exchange.

Fourth, network news executives themselves should curb the growing practice of "advocacy journalism." The experience of the last four years is that "advocacy" is being rejected, while public trust

The President and Cabinet Members

in network news is correspondingly declining. The reason is at hand: "Advocacy journalism" is premised upon the belief that, given the facts, the American people are too ignorant to reach the proper conclusion and must be led there by the hand.

Fifth, the hundreds of local television affiliates of the networks have a role to play. Just as editors of local newspapers exercise time and again, their God-given right to raise unshirted hell with the Washington AP and UPI bureaus, when an occasional piece of slanted copy comes over the wire—so, owners and editors at local stations should demand of the networks in New York and Washington that the news coverage sent over the air be objective and fair, and that the commentary be balanced.

Just as the wire services—the primary source of national and international news for hundreds of papers in scores of cities—have a special responsibility for fairness, objectivity and balance, so that same responsibility falls upon network reporters who service hundreds of stations in scores of cities.

Nor is the exercise of that responsibility all that difficult. There is no dearth of examples in Washington of newspapermen, radio and TV correspondents, and wire service reporters who, day in and day out, provide the nation with the news, even as they keep their views and opinions to themselves. Contrary to the public assertion of one famous commentator, objectivity is *not* "impossible"; with scores of journalists it is a routine achievement.

The nation's networks, the temporary custodians of airways that belong to the whole American people, are enormously lucrative enterprises. Their profits soar annually into the tens of hundreds of millions of dollars. Their principal executives have, many of them, become millionaires. Their principal personalities enjoy financial riches, prominence and prestige, not one in a hundred thousand Americans will ever come to know.

And, like the Administration, the nation does not ask a great deal in return. From the network news, it asks only comprehensiveness in coverage, objectivity in reporting, and balance in commentary.

President Nixon being sworn in by Chief Justice Burger,
1973 Inauguration

Mr. Nixon and The Court

*"The fact of the matter is . . . the balance of
power within our society has turned
dangerously against the peace forces—against
Governors and mayors and legislatures,
against the police and the courts.
The righting of this balance is the primary
business of each community and of the nation."*

—Walter Lippman
11 March 1965

ASKED ONCE HIS GREATEST MISTAKES,
President Eisenhower reportedly responded, "Two
of them are sitting on the Supreme Court."

By contrast, were President Nixon to list his
achievements, high among them would be the elevation of Justices Burger, Blackmun, Rehnquist and
Powell. If there is a matter upon which his critics
and supporters agree, it is the profound impact of
the Nixon Presidency upon the Supreme Court. The
impact was anything but accidental.

Out of office, Mr. Nixon repeatedly affirmed
his determination that, should the day come, he
would name to the Bench individuals with a judicial
philosophy not then in vogue on the Warren Court.
Invariably he would characterize such jurists as
"strict constructionists," "judicial conservatives,"
judges who will interpret the law and not make the
law. The meaning was always the same.

The genesis of the commitment was the candidate's perception of what was occurring in American
society.

During the sixties while the population rose 18% crime increased 148%.

The bromide that the answer to crime lay in elimination of its "root cause," poverty, was unconvincing. If poverty were the root cause of crime, why should crime be rising exponentially in a period of unprecedented affluence, why should the world's wealthiest democracy be among the most lawless?

In the President's judgment, the Warren Court could not escape a measure of responsibility. When society's right to be free of domestic violence was everywhere crumbling, the Supreme Court was busy discovering new "constitutional rights" of the criminally accused. "Rights" that had heretofore escaped the notice of jurists in the 700-year history of the Anglo-American system of justice.

Partially due to Court decisions which had erected a barbed wire of Dickensian legalisms about the accused, criminal trials were more and more taking on the appearance of investigations to discover police error rather than arrive at the truth and achieve justice. If justice dictates not only that the innocent go free, but that the guilty be punished, less and less was justice being done in the American criminal courts.

In his appointments to the High Court, the President's first objective, then, was to "restore balance" between the rights of the criminally accused and society's right to be secure from violence.

His second was to curb "judicial activism"—the practice of using the Constitution in general and the Fourteenth Amendment in particular to impose upon society one's own social and political views.

The President believed that the High Court was, in effect, arrogating to itself powers that rightly belonged to Congress. And he deemed it imperative that in the turbulence of modern times, far-reaching social reforms be the work of elected legislators, answerable at the polls, not of appointed judges with tenure for life, answerable only to themselves.

Mr. Nixon's determination to re-shape the Court had not escaped the attention of the incumbents. As his triumphal march through the primaries continued and the odds on a Nixon Presidency shortened, the veteran Chief Justice, Earl Warren—an old political adversary—submitted his resignation to retiring President Lyndon Johnson, to prevent the future President from naming his successor.

The ploy failed—because of the perseverance of Senator Robert Griffin of Michigan, whose tireless efforts blocked the elevation of Justice Abe Fortas to Warren's seat, an effort for which the nation would be grateful a year later, when Mr. Justice Fortas stepped down from the bench under a cloud of scandal.

Several months after Inauguration, the President announced to the nation the nomination of Federal Appellate Judge Warren Burger as Chief Justice of the United States.

With Burger elevated without difficulty, the President moved to fill the Fortas seat. Since the American South bore the burden of so many decisions, he had determined to elevate a Southern Judge. His first choice was Clement Haynsworth of the Fourth Circuit, an able, distinguished and respected jurist.

Hostile to the President's grand design to re-shape the Court, goaded by the AFL-CIO and the civil rights lobby, Senate liberals, led by Birch Bayh, collared Haynsworth, and the man after him, Judge G. Harrold Carswell, and keelhauled the two of them.

Both Judges Haynsworth and Carswell were savaged for not meeting standards of conflict of interest and judicial capacity that incumbent activists on the High Court would themselves have had difficulty in passing. Though both men had been approved by the full Senate to serve on the Federal Appellate Court, neither could pass muster for the Supreme Court.

Following Carswell's defeat, the President appeared before the White House press corps to convey a message to the Senate:

> *"Judge Carswell, and before him Judge Haynsworth have been submitted to vicious assaults on their intelligence, on their honesty, and on their character. They have been falsely charged with being racists. But when you strip away all the hypocrisy, the real reason for their rejection was their legal philosophy, a philosophy that I share, of strict construction of the Constitution, and also the accident of their birth, the fact they were born in the South."*

Though he had lost the battle, the President remained firm in purpose, and Senate liberals lost the war. The subsequent nomination of Judge Harry Blackmun of Minnesota sailed through, and two years later—after the 1970 elections modified the character of the Senate—when aging Court giants Harlan and Black resigned, the President's nominees, two brilliant strict constructionists with unimpeachable credentials, William Rehnquist and Lewis

Powell, the latter a Virginian, were elevated.

Though the "Nixon Four" is the dominant force on the Court, no public burning of the Constitution has taken place and the United States remains one of the few countries on earth where the defendants walk free on bail every afternoon, and they lock up the jury for the night.

Among the more convincing witnesses for the President's achievement is the Warren Court's principal hagiographer, the *New York Times*. In a 1972, election-eve editorial that railed against the President's "corrosive impact on the sanctity of this bedrock institution," the *Times* betrayed its anguish at the presidential success.

In ideological terms, the *Times'* position is understandable. For the President's appointments have quite nearly effected the recapture of one of the three pillars of American Government, after its loss for a generation to the liberal philosophy that guided Court decisions for a decade and a half. Not within memory had a President named four Justices in his first term; and, at the opening of his second, Mr. Nixon remained committed to the course.

In re-shaping the Supreme Court with men of his own judicial philosophy, the President had taken a page from the book of Franklin Roosevelt. Yet, publications which accepted or applauded Roosevelt's appointment of Justices sympathetic to the New Deal professed horror that Mr. Nixon would appoint Justices sympathetic to the concerns of his new majority. By 1972 the old double standard was alive and well and in the editorial offices on the Washington-New York axis. Writers who deplored Mr. Nixon's criticism of Warren Court decisions in the 1968 campaign—as undermining the American judiciary—were by 1972 using language about Burger Court decisions that would be considered intemperate by Robert Welch.

Like Justice Frankfurter, the President believed that the Warren Court moved into arenas and rendered judgments better left to the legislative arm. Nominating strict constructionists, the President hoped to shift some of those duties, those decisions, away from the Supreme Court back to where they belonged: with the Congress of the United States. Yet, some of the same commentators today championing the rights of Congress against the alleged "usurpations" of the President have demonstrated no interest whatsoever in restoring to the Congress those legislative functions seized by the Supreme Court.

Their inconsistency betrays the truth that they

The President and Philadelphia Mayor Frank Rizzo
in Independence Hall

are less concerned with where power resides than how it is used—and their sole criterion of judgment is whether it advances or retards their own ideology or social program.

Though the Supreme Court is in the President's phrase, "as balanced as I have been able to make it," all the chickens of judicial activism have not yet come home to roost.

In 1954 in *Brown versus the Board of Education,* the High Court ruled that race could no longer be a consideration in the assignment of pupils to the public schools. By 1969, it had turned 180 degrees, contending that race was the *only* constitutional consideration.

From outlawing segregation by race in 1954, the Court had moved to mandating integration by race.

As 1973 opened, among the questions to be decided was whether the Fourteenth Amendment now required that school district boundaries North and South, be abandoned and children bussed across municipal and county line, if necessary, to achieve integration. If that is what is now required, then the last legacy of the Warren Court will be an exciting decade ahead.

What the nation can expect of the Nixon Court, as it is coming to be called, is impossible to predict. Many of its decisions—such as the upholding of criminal convictions by non-unanimous juries— have been applauded by the President's supporters. A few of them—on aid to non-public schools and abortion—decidedly have not. But if there is a single characteristic which acolytes of the new Court hope will mark its era in American life, it is the characteristic of judicial restraint.

The President and Dr. Leon Sullivan, prominent black leader

Mr. Nixon and The Blacks

BETWEEN HIS FIRST AND SECOND TERMS, Mr. Nixon made dramatic inroads with every voting bloc—save one. In 1968 seven of eight black Americans voted against Richard Nixon. Four years later, seven of eight voted against his re-election.

In 1968 Candidate Nixon could not hope to compete for black votes against Hubert Humphrey, Mr. Civil Rights of the Democratic Party. But the President's 1972 opponent had no such record, no such ties, no such claim upon the allegiance of black America. The McGovern primary victories and convention success were less the work of black Democrats than of that white upper-middle class "constituency of conscience" for whom Vietnam and the environment long ago displaced civil rights in their hierarchy of concerns.

Searching for the cause of this antipathy one is hard put to find it in the statistical record. From 1969 through 1972, more de-segregation took place in Southern schools than in the fifteen previous years since *Brown versus the Board of Education.*

In the President's first term, the federal budget for civil rights enforcement rose 800% to $600 million; the Equal Employment Opportunity Commission saw its funding raised from $9 million to $46 million; Federal deposits in minority-owned banks rose from $2 million to $80 million; the percentage of minority employment in Government went from

14.1% to 19.5%, the highest ever, at a time when the total federal employment was being reduced.

For the first time, there was a black Assistant Secretary of the Navy, a black Admiral, a black Commissioner of the FCC and seven black Ambassadors. There were record numbers of blacks at the sub-Cabinet level and in the White House staff jobs.

Small business loans to minorities were boosted at the President's urging from $41 million to $435 million; an Office of Minority Business Enterprise was created; direct government purchases from minority firms jumped from $9 million to $153 million annually. The Federal contribution to black colleges doubled to $200 million.

These are not the statistics of an Administration hostile to the inclusion of black Americans into the mainstream of our national life. Yet, when black supporters of the President took this case into their communities, asking for political support, they were denounced as "sell-outs" and "Uncle Toms."

To find an adequate explanation one must look elsewhere than the record of achievement of the first Nixon Administration.

The heart of the matter seems to be that, with the changing times, most black civil rights leaders have parted company with the President on what each believes to be wise and just social policy for the whole American people. It was not always thus.

Before 1965, when the historic voting rights bill was enacted, Mr. Nixon, in and out of office, had supported every major piece of civil rights legislation presented to the Congress. Though skeptical of the apocalyptic rhetoric, the civil disobedience, the confrontation tactics, and the Utopian promises indulged in by many in the civil rights movement, he nevertheless concurred in the goals. By the end of 1965, there was in place new federal legislation guaranteeing all Americans equal access to jobs, public accommodations, the public schools, and the voting booth.

By 1969, the changing times had produced a change in demands. Now that federal courts had banned segregation in the public schools, a new demand was heard for the courts to mandate integration. Now that equal access to housing was the law of the land, the demand arose for subsidized low rent housing in middle-class and upper-class suburban communities. Now that equality of access to jobs was law, the demand came for "quotas" of jobs, and from an end to discrimination in promotion and hiring, to preferential treatment.

The old battle cry of the civil rights movement, "an equal chance at the starting line," seemed on the verge of being discarded for a new demand for an "equal place at the finish line." From equality of opportunity, the new call went forth for equality of result.

While the claims of a minority, victimized in the past, to preferential treatment is not without merit, clearly the moral arguments for the new demands are less compelling than for the old.

That black children should have the same access as whites to schools built and staffed by their own tax dollars is impossible to refute.

To assert, however that the constitutional rights of a 12-year-old Negro child are violated unless the 12-year-old child of a suburban steel worker is bussed ten miles into the city to sit beside him in class is another matter. Outlawing the evil of deny-

ing blacks equal access to teaching jobs in the public
school was just and overdue. But to inform a white
school teacher he will not get the promotion his service and talents merit because he does not meet some
racial "quota" is, again, another matter. You do not
correct an old injustice by committing a new one.

Upon issues such as these, the President and the
majority of the civil rights community appear in
fundamental disagreement. Given the belief of each
in the wisdom and rectitude of his respective posi-

Dr. Kissinger, Theodore White, members of
the White House Staff. Election day, 1972.

tion, there seems small ground for compromise, small hope for a political entente.

There are other bones of contention, present and past. Where the President had been critical of the judicial activism of the Warren Court, many black leaders viewed that intervention in the nation's social and political life as the short cut to justice. Where most black leaders almost invariably applaud new Federal social initiatives, the President had come to believe the nation, black and white, was not getting an adequate return on its social investments.

Where many civil rights leaders see the issue of bussing as the acid test of white conviction—the Nixon Administration has come to view bussing for racial balance as socially disruptive and injurious to the cause of education and racial amity alike.

To those who charge "racism" against the Administration for its opposition to bussing, the question can rightly be asked: where is the educational or social gain the nation is realizing, in the wake of all the bitterness that has been created?

One community after another, entire states, have been split apart by these court orders. Other values . . . racial peace and community tranquility, the ethnic integrity of neighborhoods, the right of parents to have their children educated near their homes . . . have been sacrificed upon the altar of racial balance. To what end? Has this produced better education for the children involved, or better relations between the races or social peace? Hardly.

If the social returns of the past decade tell us anything, it is that forced integration is an "experiment noble in purpose," unwise and unjust in application; and the time has come for the Government of the United States, executive and judicial branches alike, to remove itself altogether from this ill-advised enterprise of dictating the racial composition of schools and neighborhoods.

But if the Nixon Administration and the civil rights community cannot find common ground on quotas or compulsory integration, there are areas of common interest that need not go unexplored.

The first is the President's record in his first term, which no fair man can construe as anti-black. The second is the vested interest of the black community in not becoming captive to any single political party. The measure of hostility to the President in 1972 only served to inhibit traditional political appeals from the Republican Party, and to induce the Democratic party to take its black vote for granted.

Third, there are numerous domestic priorities of the President that correspond precisely with the needs of black America. Among these is the President's deep concern about the narcotics traffic and the rampant crime in the nation's central cities where half of black America lives. Blacks are still the primary victims of drugs and drug addicts.

Fourth, despite propaganda to the contrary, black America did not suffer economically in the Nixon years. Indeed, for blacks the first four years of the Nixon Administration were among the best four years in American history. Black income rose appreciably and the gap between black and white continued to close. Outside the South, the income of young black families where both husband and wife work now exceeds that of their white counterparts.

These statistics and facts give the lie to propaganda about a monolithic and oppressed minority within a white racist society. They say something good about America. And just as the nation deserves better of its critics, so, too, does its President.

That his social conservatism, his opposition to compulsory integration, should be opposed by civil rights leaders and their white liberal allies is understandable. That he and his Administration should therefore be written off as insensitive and bigoted is not.

Despite the election returns, there are thousands of middle-class Americans within the black community who share the President's belief in the damaging effect of welfare, the values of the work ethic, the competitive free enterprise system. Their economic interests make them natural political allies of a moderate conservative Administration like that of Richard Nixon.

And while issues of race per se may today prevent a rapprochement between the Republican Party and black America, the day is surely not too distant when other issues will again prevail.

The President and Dr. Kissinger

Foreign Policy

"Let every nation know, whether it wishes
us well or ill, that we shall pay any price, bear
any burden, meet any hardship, support
any friend, oppose any foe, in order to assure
the survival and the success of liberty."

— John F. Kennedy
Inaugural, 1961

"Without the controlling principle that the
nation must maintain its objectives and its power
in equilibrium, its purposes within its means
and its means equal to its purposes, its
commitments related to its resources and its
resources adequate to its commitments, it is
impossible to think at all about foreign affairs."

— Walter Lippmann, 1943

WHEN VICE PRESIDENT NIXON left office in 1961, the principal legacy of the Eisenhower years was a world at peace and a united America, militarily supreme. He found another world on his return in 1969.

The nation that had elected Mr. Nixon was no longer indisputably the most powerful on earth. There were new realities to recognize and deal with. While America had rested on her oars the Soviets had closed the strategic gap, and opened a broad lead in conventional weapons. There was an un-precedented Soviet presence in the Middle East, a large Soviet fleet in the Mediterranean, and a global Soviet Navy. In Central Europe, just as Khrushchev had crushed the Hungarian revolution, his successors crushed the Prague Spring. In justification of the invasion, the Soviet party chairman had announced the "Brezhnev Doctrine," a Platt Amendment for the East, asserting a Soviet right of intervention in any country where socialism was threatened. Applause for the new doctrine was as restrained in Belgrade, Bucharest and Peking—as it was in the West.

The Atlantic alliance had been strained by Vietnam, softened by affluence, weakened by neglect. The Americans were now a people divided and disillusioned over the inconclusiveness of Vietnam; and some of the nation's more articulate voices, who had urged upon the United States global responsibilities, were retreating headlong into a "new isolationism."

Ideological schism had sundered the Communist movement; and along the frontier of the People's Republic of China, her fraternal socialist ally, the Soviet Union was massing a great army. Western observers of geopolitics were hinting at the "nuclear castration" of China in a pre-emptive "surgical" strike.

Looking to mainland China, the President had concluded, well before taking office, that military containment and political ostracism no longer corresponded to the new realities.

A Communist China that sent armies into Korea, crushed Tibet, threatened war in the Formosa Strait, beat the drums for "wars of national liberation," launched the Great Leap Forward and the

Cultural Revolution, urged on the aggressor in Vietnam and humiliated India on the plains of Assam, was a fit candidate for isolation and containment. But an introspective China, groggy from excesses of the Cultural Revolution, staring northward at half a million Russian troops, and digging bomb shelters, might be one with whom we could have profitable discussions. Gazing at the new realities, the Chinese themselves had thought their way through the Leninist bombast about imperialists and their running dogs to a new world view. When a man is about to be hung in a fortnight, Dr. Johnson observed, it concentrates the mind wonderfully.

By 1969, Communist China seemed less the Church Militant of the world Communist Movement than the threatened junior partner. Taking office when the United States was confronted with two powerful adversaries—themselves at sword's point —the President concluded that it made little diplomatic sense to maintain full communication with the stronger while denying ourselves contact with the weaker.

The new realities not only dictated a new policy toward Peking but fresh and individually-tailored American policies for the separate states in the increasingly fractious Soviet empire in Eastern Europe.

Thus, just as the President made his historic visit to Peking in his first term in office, so, too, he became the first American Chief Executive to visit the Communist capitals of Rumania, Yugoslavia and Poland.

Policy changes toward the Soviet Union seemed dictated as well by the realities of 1969. Given relative strategic parity between the Great Powers, the President deemed it wise and opportune to move at once toward freezing the arms race, and toward the expansion of contact, communication and eventually trade. The possibility existed that if the Americans and Soviets could reach new agreements that were significantly and mutually beneficial, preservation of these new bonds might be an added inducement for each side to avoid potentially dangerous tensions and collisions elsewhere in the world.

NATO being crucial to the success of such an enterprise, the President, within six weeks of taking office, had toured the major capitals of Western Europe to strengthen and renew the alliance. Through exchanges of visits, regular consultation and communication, European contributions to the Western alliance were markedly increased.

In Southeast Asia where the President had inherited a war with half a million American soldiers engaged, his policy became to end American involvement without jeopardizing the cause for which the troops had been committed, and for which thousands had died. He was determined to end the war in a way that vindicated the commitments of his Democratic predecessors, and left Southeast Asia and the world closer to a just peace. To accomplish that, the President believed, South Vietnam had to be left with both the right and the wherewithal to determine its own destiny and not have an unwanted political future imposed upon it by the Communist North.

For persevering in that goal, for maintaining the credibility of the American commitment, the President was rewarded with four years of relentless

The President and Premier Chou En-Lai in China

contumely and vilification. He saw his motives questioned as immoral, his actions compared—even by men in the Congress of the United States—to those of Adolph Hitler. Though he had the support of scores of men and women in the Congress and millions in the Great Silent Majority in the country, he was hounded, badgered and harassed every step of the way out of the long and bloody conflict in Southeast Asia. Like President Lyndon Johnson before him, he was written of and spoken of, among some elements of the national liberal elite, as though he were some amoral ogre who had permanently stained the honor of his country.

Yet, as he had promised in the campagin of 1968, the President fulfilled his covenant with the American people. In late January of 1973 he announced a cease-fire in Vietnam that seemed to be a basis for a just and perhaps enduring peace. All of America's war objectives seemed to have been attained, and in retrospect all the demonstrations and denunciations of the President within the United States had served not to shorten but to prolong the war. Hanoi had agreed to settle for an honorable peace only after the election of 1972 had at last convinced them that the majority of Americans would settle for nothing less.

Crucial to that honorable peace were the two most controversial war decisions the President made as Commander-in-Chief. The first was the order to use American troops to clean out the enemy sanctuaries in occupied eastern Cambodia; the second was the President's decision of May 8, 1972, in the wake of the enemy's Easter Offensive, to renew full-scale bombing of military targets in North

Vietnam, and initiate the mining of the ports of the North.

Without these critical decisions, without the tremendous support they received from the majority of Americans, the likelihood is strong that what Americans would have today in South Vietnam is not the foundation of peace—but an on-going bloodbath, in which the victims would be all those South Vietnamese unwise enough to have placed their confidence in the word of honor of the United States.

The outlines of the new American foreign policy were first revealed in a presidential statement on Guam in July 1969. The "Nixon Doctrine," as it came to be known, reaffirmed United States determination to play the central role in the defense of freedom, but cast America's allies in stronger supporting roles.

That doctrine was both a reflection of the changed power environment, and a child of necessity. In 1945 America's future allies were economically and militarily enfeebled states and colonies. A quarter of a century later, after tens of billions in economic and military assistance to friends around the world, the United States had the right to call upon her European and Asian allies to take up responsibilities commensurate with their growing affluence and power. In the United States itself the old commitments were no longer guaranteed public support, and new questions had risen. Why, it was asked, should 200,000,000 Americans be forever responsible for the defense of 300,000,000 affluent West Europeans against 250,000,000 Russians? Since our allies have at least as great a stake in their own security and freedom as have we, thousands of miles away, why should not their military contributions be proportional to ours?

The principles behind the Nixon Doctrine were nowhere better encapsulated than in the following passage from the President's Second Inaugural:

> "We shall do our share in defending peace and freedom in the world. But we shall expect others to do their share.
>
> "The time has passed when America will make every other nation's conflict our own, or make every other nation's future our responsibility, or presume to tell the people of other nations how to manage their own affairs.
>
> "Just as we respect the right of each nation to determine its own future, we also recognize the responsibility of each nation to secure its own future.
>
> "Just as America's role is indispensable in preserving the world's peace, so is each nation's role indispensable in preserving its own peace."

By mid-1972, after the Peking and Moscow summits, even the President's political foes conceded him high marks in foreign policy. Relations with both the People's Republic of China and the Soviet Union seemed on a more solid footing. Not in the post-war era had the prospect of major war seemed more remote. Communication between East and West was mirrored in talks between the two Germanies, the two Koreas, and Pakistan and India. Though the Middle East remained a powder keg, the President and Secretary of State could claim the lion's share of credit that it had not exploded in four years, the cease-fire endured, and the search continued for a more stable peace. The coming year, 1973, was to be the Year of Europe in which East-West talks were to take place on European security, mutual and balanced force reductions, and new limits on strategic arms. Still, the four years had not been without reverses.

Despite America's exertions, her friends on Taiwan had been expelled from the UN General Assembly. Despite her diplomatic efforts, another bloody war had taken place on the sub-continent of Asia, between India and Pakistan, out of which came the new nation of Bangladesh. Though Washington-New Delhi relations were severely strained by the conflict, the New Year brought with it new hope of renewed friendly ties between the largest democracy in the East and the largest in the West.

Between the Superpowers, however, at least three incidents had occurred which seemed even more ominous. In 1970, the Soviet supported the Syrian invasion of Jordan which pushed the Middle East back toward crisis; then tested American resolve in the Caribbean with moves that looked toward establishment of a strategic submarine base in Cuba.

In early 1972, as the Vietnam war seemed to be withering away, the North Vietnamese launched their Easter offensive, sending virtually their entire army across the DMZ in an effort to overturn the successes of Vietnamization. That invasion could not have taken place without massive infusions of Russian armor, artillery and anti-aircraft, and the severity and magnitude of the offensive threatened the U.S.-Soviet summit.

On each occasion the President's diplomatic and military response made clear that detente requires restraint upon both sides, that Soviet challenges would be met. The President's answer to Hanoi's invasion of the South was the renewed bombing of the North and the mining of its harbors. Two weeks later, with the invasion broken at An Loc, Hue and Kontum, the President was in Moscow.

But the spirit of detente that existed between the governments of East and West clearly had not penetrated downward from the Kremlin.

If the testimony of Russian Jews, Ukrainian Christians and dissident intellectuals could be believed, Soviet enthusiasm for Western computers, Ford trucks and Midwest wheat did not extend to Western ideals. And there remained a grave, unanswered question for the future.

When Tito passed on, what would happen to Yugoslavia under the centrifugal pressures of nationalism? How would the Soviets respond? Did their on-going buildup in strategic and conventional arms, post-SALT, portend a Soviet drive to move beyond parity to strategic supremacy, to seize the diplomatic and political leverage superiority might provide?

Would the new detente last longer than the evident Soviet need for American grain and the latest in Western technology?

How would the West react if China after Mao abandoned its new relationship with the democratic West and settled its territorial and ideological quarrel with the Communist east, to present again to the world a united front?

At home, though the Pentagon share of the national budget and GNP was—in a time of unprecedented abundance—the lowest in decades, voices in Congress were contending that even the present budget was excessive.

To the President, the hope of a "generation of peace" hinged upon American willingness to maintain a military deterrent second to none. To his critics, the "generation of peace" was a golden opportunity to dismantle the deterrent, to set a good example for the Soviets, to unilaterally beat our swords into plowshares.

This division in government reflected among the people was among the more relevant realities of the new decade; for, as Walter Lippmann wrote at the height of the Second World War:

> ". . . when a people is divided within itself about the conduct of its foreign relations, it is unable to agree on the determination of its true interest. It is unable to prepare adequately for war or to safeguard successfully its peace. Thus, its course in foreign affairs depends, in Hamilton's words, not on reflection and choice, but on accident and force."

"All the News That's Fit to Print"

The New York Times

LATE CITY EDITION

Weather: Cloudy, rain likely today and tonight. Cloudy, cool tomorrow. Temp. range: today 48-60; Tuesday 45-61. Full U.S. report on Page 93.

VOL. CXXII . . . . No. 41,927 NEW YORK, WEDNESDAY, NOVEMBER 8, 1972 15 CENTS

NIXON ELECTED IN LANDSLIDE; M'GOVERN IS BEATEN IN STATE; DEMOCRATS RETAIN CONGRESS

President's Margin Seen As a Million in the State

By FRANK LYNN

President Nixon swept New York State yesterday and was running ahead of Senator McGovern in New York City with a third of the vote counted.

The President won handily in Queens and on Staten Island, was running neck-and-neck in Brooklyn and was trailing in Manhattan and the Bronx.

His statewide plurality was expected to exceed a million votes.

The President's strong showing in the state rivaled the 1956 victory of President Dwight D. Eisenhower, who first brought Mr. Nixon to the national ticket 20 years ago.

The Nixon victory did not appear to carry too far down the Republican line. The Legislature remained Republican, but with no indication of substantially increased Republican majorities.

Three Republican candidates for the Court of Appeals held slight leads but returns were still inconclusive.

A Nixon victory in New York City would make him the first Republican Presidential candidate to win the city since Calvin Coolidge did so in 1924.

The President's capture of the state was only the third time a Republican Presidential candidate had won New York since 1928.

Dozens of sample districts showed last night that the President substantially improved his 1968 showing in virtually all ethnic groups and geographic areas in the state and city.

In many cases, particularly in the cities, Mr. Nixon surpassed Governor Rockefeller's victory margins of two years ago.

In New York City, Senator McGovern carried districts that were predominantly black, Puerto Rican and Jewish. But in the Jewish areas, Mr. Nixon doubled his showing of four years before. In a middle class

Continued on Page 36, Column 2

MANY VOTES SPLIT

Miller of Iowa Loses in an Upset—G.O.P. Makes Some Gains

By R. W. APPLE Jr.

The Democratic party retained control of the Senate and the House of Representatives yesterday in the face of President Nixon's smashing victory as voters in all parts of the nation split tickets in vast numbers.

The Democrats took at least two previously Republican seats in the Senate, scoring a mild upset in Kentucky and a startling one in Iowa. That offset early Republican pickups in two Southwestern states—Oklahoma and New Mexico.

With returns inconclusive in a dozen states, the Democrats had won 10 Senate contests. Together with their 41 holdover seats, that assured them control when Congress convenes on Jan. 3.

May Gain 12 Seats

The figures for the House were far less complete, but the Republicans were not making the gains they needed to win control.

It appeared probable that Republican gains in the Senate would be held to one or, at the most, two seats, and in the House to no more than 12.

The present Senate line-up is 54 Democrats, 44 Republicans, one Conservative-Republican and one independent who votes with the Democrats. In the House it is 255 Democrats, 177 Republicans and three vacancies.

Survive the Landslide

Mr. Nixon's coattails proved relatively short this year, as they had in 1968. In state after state, he swept to massive victories while Republican candidates for the Senate were defeated, as in Kentucky, Rhode Island, Georgia. Nor was the President able to give much aid to House nominees.

Such Democratic Representatives as Romano T. Mazzoli in Kentucky, Ella T. Grasso in Connecticut, Henry Helstoski in New Jersey and John Brademas in Indiana were heavily re-elected. All had been considered vulnerable to a Nixon land-

Continued on Page 24, Column 7

President and Mrs. Nixon arriving in Washington and Vice President Agnew voting in Maryland yesterday

Associated Press

MARGIN ABOUT 60%

Triumph of President Extends to Every Area of Nation

By MAX FRANKEL

Richard Milhous Nixon won re-election by a huge majority yesterday, perhaps the largest ever given a President.

Mr. Nixon scored a stunning personal triumph in all sections of the country, sweeping New York and most other bastions of Democratic strength.

He was gathering more than 60 per cent of the nation's ballots, a trend that could bring him more than 500 electoral votes. The victory was reminiscent of the landslide triumphs of Franklin D. Roosevelt in 1936 and Lyndon B. Johnson in 1964, although it could fall just short of their record proportions.

Tickets Are Split

Despite this drubbing of George Stanley McGovern, the Democratic challenger, the voters split their tickets in record numbers to leave the Democrats in control of both houses of Congress and a majority of the nation's governorships. Mr. Nixon thus became the first two-term President to face an opposition Congress at both inaugurals.

The President seemed certain, however, to claim a clear mandate for his policies of gradual disengagement from Vietnam, continued strong spending on defense, opposition to busing to integrate the schools and a slowdown in Federal spending for social programs. These are the issues he stressed through the campaign.

The 59-year-old Mr. Nixon, who will be 60 before inauguration on Jan. 20, could also claim a resounding personal vindication against the strong charges of corruption brought against him personally by the opposition.

By coincidence, the greatest triumph of his 26 years in national politics came on the 10th anniversary of his defeat for Governor of California—the night he told newsmen they would not have Nixon to kick around anymore.

McGovern Concedes

Mr. McGovern, 50, conceded defeat before midnight in the East with a telegram of support for the President if he leads the nation to peace abroad and justice at home.

The South Dakotan took credit for helping to push the Administration nearer to peace in Indochina and assured his cheering supporters that their defeat would bear fruit for years to come.

The President responded in a brief address from the White House, expressing appreciation to his supporters and respect for the supporters of Mr. McGovern, whose name he pronounced for the first time in months. He promised rapid progress toward peace and prosperity.

Mr. Nixon carried into office again his running mate, Vice President Spiro Theodore Agnew, who will now be regarded as a formidable candidate for the Republican Presidential nomination four years hence.

His opponent, Robert Sargent

President Has Big Margin In Jersey and Connecticut

Case Big Winner

By RONALD SULLIVAN

President Nixon won the overwhelming victory predicted for him in New Jersey in yesterday's Presidential election, defeating Senator George McGovern by a 2-to-1 margin.

At the same time, Senator Clifford P. Case, the liberal Republican, won a fourth term and one of the biggest Senate election victories in New Jersey's history, defeating Paul J. Krebs, the Democratic candidate.

However, incumbent Democratic Representatives survived the G.O.P. onslaught at the top of the ballot in what political leaders described as a remarkable display of ticket-splitting.

With both Mr. Nixon and Senator Case piling up 2-to-1 margins throughout the state, Republican leaders predicted that the President's margin would rival the 800,000-vote plurality achieved by Dwight D. Eisenhower in the 1956 Republican sweep.

Moreover, the Nixon and Case victories were uniform, with both candidates winning at least 20 of New Jersey's 21 counties. Only in Hudson, where the polls closed at 11 P.M., was the issue in doubt.

For Mr. Nixon, his New

Continued on Page 37, Column 3

Hartford Senate G.O.P.

By LAWRENCE FELLOWS

Special to The New York Times

HARTFORD, Nov. 7—President Nixon carried Connecticut today in a landslide victory.

The President swept the state's eight electoral votes with a plurality of about 240,000, approaching the huge margin by which the late President Dwight D. Eisenhower carried the state in 1956, the last time a Republican Presidential candidate won here.

With 165 of the 169 towns in the state reporting, the Presidential tally was:

Nixon	731,086
McGovern	491,968

The Republicans also took control of the State Senate, and stood a good chance of winning the House of Representatives. But widespread ticket-splitting enabled three of the incumbent Democratic Representatives to keep their

Continued on Page 37, Column 7

M'GOVERN OFFERS SUPPORT TO NIXON

Senator Concedes Election —Voices Hope for Peace and Justice for 4 Years

By JAMES M. NAUGHTON

Special to The New York Times

SIOUX FALLS, S.D., Nov. 7—Senator George McGovern conceded the election to President Nixon tonight and offered him his support for the next four years.

Appearing on television, he told his supporters he had sent a telegram to the President congratulating him on his victory.

"I hope," he said in the telegram, "that in the next four years you will lead us to a time of peace abroad and justice at home."

Earlier the Senator awaited returns as the Nixon landslide rumbled through South Dakota on its way from one coast to the other.

Aides to the Democratic Presidential nominee reported that he had taken a nap not long after the polls closed in most of the nation. The eighth floor of the Holiday Inn, where Mr. McGovern and his wife, Eleanor, waited for the voters' verdict, was sealed off by

Continued on Page 2, Column 3

The Election at a Glance

President

Needed for Election—270 Electoral Votes

	*Number of States	Electoral Votes
Nixon	28	362
McGovern	2	17
In Doubt	21	159

The Senate

Newly Elected Senators		Make-up of New Senate	
Democrats	10	Democrats	51
Republicans	11	Republicans	37
In Doubt	12	In Doubt	12

The House

Democrats Elected	75
Republicans Elected	33
In Doubt	327

*Includes District of Columbia.

NIXON ISSUES CALL TO WORK TOGETHER

Asks Backers and Opponents to Help Achieve Nation's 'Common Great Goals'

By ROBERT B. SEMPLE Jr.

Special to The New York Times

WASHINGTON, Nov. 7—President Nixon summoned his supporters and political opponents tonight to "work together" in the four years ahead to achieve "our common great goals."

In a brief statement from the Oval Office of the White House on television only a few minutes after he had received a telegram conceding defeat from Senator George McGovern of South Dakota, Mr. Nixon thanked the nation for its overwhelming support at the polls, but said that the landslide itself would mean nothing unless it could be translated into "a victory for America."

The President mentioned three major goals. The first was peace in Vietnam and continuing improvement in relationships with the Communist world.

The second was prosperity without war, and the third was equal opportunity for all Americans regardless of background.

Continued on Page 24, Column 3

Victory, 10 Years Later

Spectacular Nixon Vote Considered Vindication in Light of Past Defeats

By JAMES RESTON

News Analysis

It was a spectacular personal victory for Richard Nixon, 10 years to the day, and almost to the hour, after his most humiliating defeat by Pat Brown in the 1962 election for the governorship of California.

Beaten by John Kennedy by the narrowest of margins in the Presidential election of 1960, beaten again for the control of his own state in 1962, finished with American politics by his own angry proclamation exactly a decade ago, here he is now, not only vindicated but triumphant in one of the most decisive victories in the history of American Presidential politics.

In a few days before he will take the oath of office for a second term as President of the United States (Jan. 20), he will be 60 years old. His thirties were a political surprise, even to himself, his forties were an agony of controversy and self-doubt, his fifties were a struggle and at the end a triumph. What now will he do with his sixties? This is the question that even his most intimate associates in Washing-

Japan and the Common Market countries of Europe, who are now challenging the American economic leadership of the modern world.

At home, Mr. Nixon has to deal also now with the minorities who failed to support him in the election: the poor and the blacks who have been left behind in the general prosperity of the nation, the young in the universities who have been over-run but not persuaded or

Continued on Page 34, Column 2

Bella Abzug Wins Easily; Reid Leads as Democrat

By RICHARD L. MADDEN

Representative Bella S. Abzug, a one-term Manhattan Democrat, won a decisive re-election victory yesterday, while Representative Ogden R. Reid, a former Republican, led in his bid to win re-election as a Democrat in Westchester County.

In another key Westchester race, Representative Peter A. Peyser, a freshman Republican, led his predecessor in the House, Richard L. Ottinger, a Democrat-Liberal who was seeking to recapture his former seat.

Mrs. Abzug defeated Mrs. Priscilla M. Ryan, a Liberal and widow of the late Representative William F. Ryan, who had defeated Mrs. Abzug in the

half the voted counted was Representative John G. Dow of Newburgh, a liberal Democrat who has won three terms in the relatively conservative area of Rockland and Orange Counties. The leader in the race was Assemblyman Benjamin A. Gilman, a Middletown Republican.

But an upstate Democrat who had been a prime target of Republican campaign strategists, Representative James M. Hanley, a four-term Democrat from Syracuse, was holding a substantial lead over Leonard C. Koldin, his Republican-Conservative opponent.

Two incumbent Long Island Democrats who had faced strong opposition maintained leads with about half the votes

Remote Pickups Cut By C.B.S. in Strike

By ALBIN KREBS

The Columbia Broadcasting System was forced last night to drop from its election coverage most pickups from points outside its studios because of the continuing strike of its cameramen, audio engineers and other technicians.

For a time yesterday, it appeared that picket lines established by the C.B.S. workers at pooled facilities would be honored by employes of the two

A Rockefeller Loses West Virginia Race

By BEN A. FRANKLIN

Special to The New York Times

CHARLESTON, W.Va., Nov. 7 — Gov. Arch A. Moore Jr. was re-elected to a second term tonight, defeating Secretary of State John D. Rockefeller 4th, in a race that was nationally watched for indications of a Rockefeller future in national politics.

President Nixon won the state's six electoral votes with more than 60 per cent of the

Summary of Other News

Following is a summary of major nonelection news. A full report begins on the first page, second part.

Canarsie School Boycott

Leaders of Canarsie parents who have kept their children out of school for two weeks declared yesterday that "the boycott is over" and called on parents to return their children to school. But the prospect of full classes today remained in doubt since more than 1,000 parents shouted down the same call Monday night.

Bid by Vietcong

Agents of the National Liberation Front have made several recent contacts with Saigon's anti-Government, non-Communist opposition, according to opposition sources.

Britons Protest Price Rises

The New American Majority

IN FASHIONING THE GREAT LANDSLIDE OF 1972, two dates stand out. The first is August 15, 1971, when the President's announcement of his New Economic Policy shocked the economy out of its lassitude and stanched Administration hemorrhaging on its most vulnerable issue. The second was May 8, 1972, when the President announced renewed bombing of North Vietnam and the mining of its harbors, assuring his enlarged constituency that the United States was not coming out of Southeast Asia "on the skids," and making Vietnam the President's "issue", not that of his opposition. Following those actions, pollsters and analysts reversed earlier predictions and made the President a heavy favorite against any Democratic opponent.

But a victory is not a landslide. And if the President entered the summer of '72 holding two high pair, the Democratic Convention dealt him the full house. They nominated George McGovern.

Contrary to the post-election mythology, the vulnerability of a McGovern candidacy was less the man himself than his beliefs. No Jennings Bryan or Jack Kennedy, George McGovern nevertheless brought to a national campaign impressive assets.

When, we were told, the nation was tired of familiar faces, his was new. When, we were told, the country was fed up with politics as usual, here was an unconventional politician, an outsider who had carried the day against the party hacks, a Prairie Populist who had won his nomination in the primaries, not some compromise candidate chosen in a smoke-filled room.

"... (George McGovern) will appeal to the unrich, unpowerful and unprivileged majority, and, therefore, he will be elected," declared J.K. Galbraith, July 1, 1972.

When, we were told, twenty-five million new voters stood poised to deliver the *coup de main* to the old order, here was the candidate of the "New Politics" who echoed the anti-war sentiments and anti-establishment views ascribed to the young.

"... he (Richard Nixon) needs six or seven million new votes if he is to offset not just McGovern gains in formerly Republican areas, but above all, the Democratic potentiality among first voters. ... The Republican plurality of 600,000 four years ago could sink without a trace in this flood of new votes."

Thus spake Arthur Schlesinger in the *New York Times,* July 30, 1972 and, as living, marching proof that McGovern had captured the youth of America, there was his army of volunteers that was the envy of his opposition and the darling of the press.

It was the man's ideology, not his personality or competence, that had Republicans making novenas for his nomination and frantic Democrats urging him to move to the center while there was yet time. His political philosophy was the albatross that hung about his neck.

Hubert Humphrey, the seasoned campaigner, was the first to probe successfully the weakness in the California primary. Within ten days, his assaults upon McGovern defense and welfare positions had cut fifteen points out of McGovern's lead, and turned the predicted McGovern avalanche into a narrow victory. But the most convincing evidence of the weakness of his positions was the post-nomination gyrations of Mr. McGovern himself.

One is hard put to name a single issue—from amnesty, to abortion, to marijuana, to troops in Thailand, to POWs, to space, to welfare—where George McGovern did not trim or qualify or abandon altogether. Tom Eagleton was not the only cargo put over the side in the general election.

The most damning evidence that the "New Politics" of ultraliberal ideology and issues was opposed by a majority of Americans was that, when the crunch came, the chosen champion of the "New Politics" abandoned his ground for the old politics of bread-and-butter, the traditional strategy of Democratic nominees from Roosevelt to Humphrey.

But the "New American Majority" that swept the President back into office was years, not weeks, in the making.

In economic terms, its backbone is working class and middle class. Geographically and electorally, its base is in the Southern and Border states, the Mountain states and Midwest. But, against an ideological leftist, it was strong enough to carry every state in the Union save Massachusetts.

Socially and culturally, it is traditional America, "Middle America," as opposed to the liberal elite, the constituency of conscience, the counterculture. In terms of the old Roosevelt coalition, it is the Republican political base wedded to the "Solid South," the farm vote and half the Catholic, ethnic and blue-collar vote of the big cities.

Defined by the central issue of our time, Vietnam, it is the majority that stood for an end to the war in Vietnam, but not peace on Communist terms.

Its membership was described by Mr. Nixon at the 1968 Republican Convention as the *"forgotten Americans, the non-shouters, the non-demonstrators . . . good people . . . decent people . . . they work and they save and they pay their taxes and they care. . . ."*

If the "New American Majority" becomes the successor to the Roosevelt coalition, it will be an historic achievement. Eight years ago, when the blueprints began to take shape, a less likely architect and contractor than Republican Richard Nixon could not have been imagined.

The 1964 coup at the Cow Palace had left the Republican Party divided, feuding and plunging inexorably toward one of the great disasters of modern politics. Though he did not share the undiluted conservatism of Barry Goldwater, though realistic enough to see the abyss toward which they were headed, Richard Nixon nevertheless marched as a loyal soldier in the ranks.

The candidate himself barely did more for his doomed party. Election day, as predicted, summoned up memories of Alf Landon. Barry Goldwater was defeated by 15 million votes; Republican strength in the Senate was sheared to 32; in the House to 140; the number of Republican Governors plunged to 17 and the loss of 500 Republican legislators left the party in control of but six of the fifty state legislatures.

In November, 1964, the question was not when

the Republicans would come back, but whether they would survive.

Among the survivors, only the former Vice President had the prestige to begin the re-building and a passport valid in both wings of the party. So, in January 1965, he began, simultaneously, two of the great salvage operations of American politics —picking up the pieces of his shattered career, and re-building his ruined party.

Traveling to more than 40 states in two years, coaxing Republicans of all shades into the '66 race, raising an estimated five-million-dollar war chest, brokering alliances and truces between conservatives and liberals, sharpening the issues against Lyndon Johnson, Mr. Nixon led his party to its greatest off-year triumph since 1946. He had predicted almost precisely the gains Republicans would make. Forty House seats, three Senate seats, eight Governorships and 700 state legislators, he promised; and that was nearly an exact description of what November 8th delivered.

Though he won a measure of credit for his efforts, press attention quickly turned toward 1968, and the new galaxy of Republican stars—Rockefeller, Percy, Reagan, Hatfield, Brooke and Romney —whose faces graced the post-election covers of *Time* and *Newsweek*.

Following the election, Mr. Nixon retired from active politics for six months to intensify his re-education in foreign policy, journeying 100,000 miles to four continents and some 30 nations. On his return, he made his decision to contest the Republican nomination by entering the "fires of the primaries."

Two operative principles were paramount in

that campaign: First, enter every contested primary to convince a GOP certain of his ability but skeptical of his appeal that he was not a "loser;" secondly, campaign in such a fashion that, post-convention, no Republican, liberal or conservative, had grounds to take a walk, as happened in 1964.

The primary campaign was a text book operation; the nomination won on the first ballot, and the party united for the fall of 1968, as it had not been in decades.

But by 1968, even a unified Republican Party could claim the allegiance of but a fourth of the people. Victory in November required the support of an overwhelming majority of Independents and the defection of millions of Democrats. To win these last, the President fixed his sights upon the Solid South, and the ethnic and working class precincts of the North and Midwest.

In appealing to alienated Southerners and Northern ethnics, the Republicans were not without competition. Sandwiched between that lightning rod of Southern grievance and blue-collar disenchantment, George Wallace, and the bread-and-butter politics of Hubert Humphrey and the AFL-CIO, Richard Nixon barely squeezed through with 43% of the vote.

Undeterred by his narrow margin, the President, hard upon taking office, launched a second campaign to build the "new majority." Fortunately, his principal allies were the national Democratic Party and the liberal establishment.

First courted was the Old Confederacy. Fed up with a decade of sanctimonious rhetoric from the scribes and Pharisees of the Northeast, the South found, in the President's visible patriotism, his eco-

The President and Governor John B. Connally

nomic conservatism, his belief in state's rights, his court appointments, his commitment to "equal treatment" for all sections of the country, initiatives to applaud.

Early Presidential decisions that had liberal editorial writers lunging for their typewriters caused Southerners to conclude that this Nixon-Agnew team was more to their liking than the Hickory Hill Jet Set and the Wisconsin Avenue boulevardiers.

Though his critics were crying "Southern Strategy," the President's politics and policy decisions were not going unnoticed in the Catholic and ethnic communities of the North, East and Midwest, as well as Dixie.

By 1969, the most serious political rupture in the nation was not between Republicans and Democrats, but between the lower and middle class Democratic center and right, and its upper-middle-class elite and left. To suggest that the President's gains among Catholics came on the abortion issue or aid to non-public schools is as simplistic and mistaken as to attribute his enormous gains in the South to Haynsworth and Carswell.

There exists a range of issues, a panoply of concerns and attitudes, where the President and socially conservative Democrats are aligned on one side, and liberal Democrats on the other.

Where the former believe in punishing returning draft-dodgers who ran away to Canada and Sweden, the liberal establishment calls for amnesty. Where the former are visibly patriotic and applaud the President for holding out for a "peace with honor," the latter view flag-waving as a fetish of the simple-minded and consider the President next to immoral for not having accepted a coalition government with the Communists.

Where conservatives believe wealthy liberals are hypocrites for sending their children to lily-white academies while forcing bussing down the throats of the working class, the latter think the conservative working class among the more reactionary and bigoted segments in American life, hostile to black progress after they have gotten "theirs." The former would like the porno shops shut down and their proprietors horsewhipped; the latter warn against the ugly specter of censorship. The former is outraged and frightened by crime in the streets; the latter is more concerned with "root causes" of crime, the "rights of defendants" and conditions in the prisons. The one believes the death penalty a useful deterrent, the other an abomination.

On and on, the issues could be enumerated. The ideological fault that runs beneath the surface and down the center of the Democratic Party is as deep as any political division in America. From their respective views on the military, marijuana, school prayer, welfare, campus disorders, the "Greening of America," George Wallace, civil disobedience, foreign aid, the United Nations — the Catholic and ethnic and Southern conservative foot soldiers who gave FDR those great landslides are in fundamental disagreement with the isolated, intellectual aristocracy and liberal elite who now set the course of their party. While the Nixon landslide was a victory of the man over McGovern, it was also a victory of "the New American Majority" over the "New Politics," a victory of traditional American values and beliefs over the claims of the "counter-culture," a victory of "Middle America" over the celebrants of Woodstock Nation.

This reality makes the long-predicted "realignment of parties" a possibility, and could make Mr. Nixon the Republican FDR.

Aware of the political and cultural collisions shattering the majority coalition, the President has long been hunting where the ducks are.

For four years he conspicuously courted union support, and this policy, along with sharing the same foxhole on the issue of Vietnam, produced after four years, a mutual respect and confidence where none had existed before. And the Republican whose nomination in 1968 had generated for Hubert Humphrey the greatest AFL-CIO election effort ever, emerged in 1972 with the open support or benevolent neutrality of more unions and labor leaders than any Republican in history.

Still another voting bloc where the President made historic gains was the American Jewish community.

Again, it was a spectrum, not a single issue, that nearly tripled the President's vote within four years. First, there was his proven record of support for Israeli security, measured against the McGovern plan to moth ball half of the United States Sixth Fleet. Second, there was the President's foreign policy experience and long record of anti-Communism, now an asset among American Jews angry at Soviet maltreatment of Russian Jews and shocked by Soviet diplomatic conduct in the days preceding the Six Day War. Third, there was concern over the "quotas" associated with McGovern, which could be imposed upon teaching, the civil service and higher education only at the expense of American

Jews. Fourth, there was the consternation among Jewish businessmen, bankers, doctors and lawyers, who saw the McGovern schemes to limit inheritance, impose confiscatory taxes, and re-distribute income as programs that would disproportionately punish successful Jewish Americans who had finally reached their day in the sun. Fifth, in the Jewish communities in Manhattan and Brooklyn, among shopkeepers, teachers, social workers and taxi drivers, the President's tough stance on crime and narcotics seemed more in accord with reality than the permissiveness identified with George McGovern. "Law and order" can be ridiculed as a code word for racism in the security of the Harvard Faculty Club, but in the Jewish communities of Manhattan and Brooklyn, it is the missing ingredient of civilized life. Sixth, some black militants and the devotees of the New Left who hovered about the fringe of the McGovern camp had manifested, at times, not only anti-Israeli, but anti-Semitic sentiments.

In four years, Mr. Nixon had convinced tens of thousands of American Jews that the Old Left myths about Richard Nixon, dating to the days of Alger Hiss, must have been just that—myths.

High on the list of the remaining questions his Presidency will answer is whether Richard Nixon can breathe life into his "New American Majority" and set it upon the vacant throne of American politics left by the Roosevelt Coalition.

There are similarities between the opportunities of 1932 and 1972, but also crucial differences.

Though both Presidents Roosevelt and Nixon have earned and received the unvarnished hostility of the establishments they de-throned — in FDR's case, Big Business and Wall Street, in Mr. Nixon's the Liberal Establishment—FDR was more fortunate in that his opposition was not only discredited in the eyes of the nation, but inarticulate in its own defense. When FDR railed in 1937 against those "who have profaned the temple of our civilization," he was kicking a toothless and dying lion.

Despite his enormous landslide, Mr. Nixon's opposition is neither humbled nor inarticulate. It still dominates the public dialogue; it can yet claim the allegiance of the most educated and articulate segments of American life. Though rejected in 1968 and 1972, political liberalism remains the reigning ideology in the high culture of the nation and a strongly competing force in its political life.

Liberals still dominate the Senate, the great foundations, the national media, the prestige universities, the arts. They publish and promote and review most of the books the nation buys and reads. They are not without power. As Mr. Broder reminds us, these are "the men and the movement that broke Lyndon B. Johnson's authority."

So, the problem simply stated is that the Lords Spiritual and the Lords Temporal in the society are at sword's point. The men of words distrust and oppose the men of action, and the sentiment is warmly reciprocated. The President who has won the allegiance of the majority of Americans has confidence in himself and his leadership, but has no great Establishment behind him—in Dr. Moynihan's phrase, no "second and third orders of advocacy." And the Liberal Establishment, which has the assets, the ability and the experience to lead, has lost the allegiance of the common man, and that confidence in itself without which no great thing can be accomplished.

As the President moved into his second term, a new collision seemed assured. This time, the issue was not Vietnam, as in the first Administration, but the role of the national government in American life.

Supported by his new majority, the President believed that the time had come to reverse the trend of forty years, to begin reducing the relative size and role of the Federal Government, to begin restoring power, responsibility and resources to states and cities and communities, and to the people whence it had come.

"We have lived too long with the consequences of attempting to gather all power and responsibility in Washington . . . the time has come to turn away from the condescending policies of paternalism. . . ."

That declaration of conviction and belief was contained in President Nixon's Second Inaugural Address, and, if doubts of his resolution remained on Capitol Hill, they evaporated with the submission of his Federal Budget. The die was cast. A collision between Congress and President, between the nation's regnant ideology on one hand and the nation's political majority on the other, seemed assured.

But the outcome of the debate, the result of that collision, need not necessarily be politically unhealthy or unfruitful for the United States.

The Nixon Legacy

In the final year of the Nixon Presidency, 1976, the United States closes her second century of independence, and sets out upon the third. At midpassage, the outlines of the legacy that the Nixon Administration hopes to leave become discernible.

First: An honorable end to American involvement in the war in Vietnam, a peace that does not disgrace the sacrifices of a decade. In the first month of the President's second term that seemed to have been achieved. A cease-fire appeared in place; an agreement had been initialed and signed that held the promise of a more enduring peace; and American prisoners were on the way home.

Secondly, the President hoped to build a new structure of relations between the Great Powers, to erect the scaffolding of a more secure peace and a more stable planet. This called for the strengthening of America's ties with friendly nations and continued contact and communication with her adversaries.

Further, the President intended that his second term would bring new East-West agreements regarding the disposition of military forces in Europe, and expanded agreement on control of nuclear arms.

The achievement of these objectives, however, requires renewed recognition by Americans that their military establishment is not some costly and unnecessary evil but the bulwark of global security and Western freedom. The nation's armed forces suffered in Vietnam wounds that cannot be healed by comparability in pay. Anti-war sentiment spilled over into anti-military sentiment. What Americans once proudly termed the "Great Arsenal of Democracy" is now disparagingly termed by many the "Military-Industrial Complex" and in fashionable circles, the professional military was, by 1972, being derided as the more benighted half. Americans would do well to recall in these times that nations which treat their soldiers as second-class citizens have a history of falling prey to nations that do not.

Among the President's domestic concerns, when he first took office, few ranked higher than the "Cooling of America." The year 1968 had been marked by disorder, acrimony and violence, as few others in American history. By 1972, however, the year 1968 seemed decades away, and though many were reluctant to credit the President with the new calm, there was little question who would have been blamed had it not come about.

With the return of American troops and prisoners from the war zone, there was added reason to hope the nation may have entered a new era. While sharp differences remained between the President and his political opponents on matters of philosophy, national priorities and public policy, there was hope that these differences could be debated, these positions could be contested, without the venomous rhetoric that marked the debate over Vietnam.

One of those issues of sharpest disagreement remains the President's determination to re-shape the Supreme Court. Given the successes in his first term, the likelihood is good that one of the monuments of the Nixon Presidency will be what historians characterize as the "Nixon Court."

Economically, the President's ambition is the same goal that eluded him in the first term: full employment without inflation and without war, a situation the nation has not known in almost two decades.

With American military involvement in Vietnam ending, with economists predicting a boom year, the prospects for achievement never seemed better than in January of 1973. But realization of that goal forced the President to make a painful political choice. Faced with mounting deficits stretching into the distant future, the President, to curb inflation, had either to raise federal taxes or cut federal spending. The latter choice was dictated by his personal philosophy, his experience in office, and the will of the American people as expressed in the November returns.

By 1973, enough evidence had been gathered on the Great Society programs to return an indictment. Those most committed to the costly social innovations enacted in the sixties were by January, 1973, apologetic, defensive and disappointed at their enormous expense and manifest unsuccess. Those who had opposed the Great Society spending as wasteful and inefficacious were now charging, and not without merit, that programs designed for the poor, and paid for by the working and middle class, were primarily benefitting an upper-middle class elite of specialists, consultants, bureaucrats, academics, sociologists, educationists and poverty concessionaires. There was indeed a "redistribution of income" taking place, but not the one most Americans had in mind when they supported the Great Society. The tax dollars of working America were being funneled into the pockets of a more affluent professional class—in the name of the poor. Surely, a wholesale rip-off of American taxpayers and working people to feather the nest of a new Poverty-Education Industrial Complex, was not what Lyndon Johnson had in mind when he stood before Congress and declared, "We Shall Overcome."

"He has erected a multitude of New Offices and sent hither swarms of Officers to harass our people and eat out their substance." That indictment of George III in the Declaration of Independence would not be an altogether inaccurate epitaph for what became the Great Society.

Americans had been promised in those years, that if only our people were generous enough and trusting enough, the new social engineers would end poverty, improve the quality of education, provide housing for the poor, take care of the sick, and lead us to the New Jerusalem.

Today, what progress has been made has been largely the fruit of the much maligned free enterprise system, and we are far from the promised sunny uplands. Disillusionment with Government programs has replaced hope. And taxpayers ask: Where have all the billions gone?

Though fashionable today to denigrate NASA's magnificent achievement of sending a man to the moon and bringing him back again within a decade, at least the U.S. space and scientific teams succeeded splendidly in their assignment, while their counterparts in the social agencies failed and failed miserably—and not for lack of funds.

Contrary to the Galbraithian mythology about a private sector filthy rich and a public sector starved for funds, the last ten years have been the salad days of the public sector. Federal civilian expenditures as a percentage of GNP have doubled; much the same is true at state and local levels. The Great Society that began at $1 billion annually was by 1972 costing $34 billion annually. And is there an American around — other than the professionals carving up the pie—who believes the taxpayer is getting a dollar's worth of goods for his dollar of tax?

A case in point is American education. In the past ten years, the cost of elementary and secondary education has doubled; the average expenditure per pupil is three or four times what it was when most adult Americans were going to school. And what have Americans received in return for these tens of billions? A public school system in which the quality of education and the level of learning are plunging in city after city.

New school buildings, higher teacher salaries, lower pupil-teacher ratios, higher expenditures per student, may all be things desirable in and of themselves. But experience indicates they have little to do with improving the education of children.

In recent years, the education lobby has been given all it has asked and more—and it has not delivered the goods. The horse sense of the angry majorities voting down one school bond issue after another can hardly be faulted.

Nor is education the lone example. Has there really been a dramatic increase in the quality of housing for the poor commensurate with the billions of tax dollars invested in these programs? While urban renewal wiped out tens of thousands of dwellings of the poor, the replacement housing—built at great cost—seems to have benefited primarily the contractors, the builders and the middle class. Though smaller and smaller percentages of Americans can be classified as impoverished, the platoons of poverty warriors seem to grow and grow. America is an affluent nation, Americans a generous people. But the day is past when Americans can or will approve in silence the expenditure of more billions of their tax dollars, when they see little or no return at the end of the line. And the matter is only exacerbated as they see tens of thousands of those dollars used to subsidize militants and radicals who specialize in social heroics and street confrontations with local or federal officials. The tax revolution sweeping the nation is a cause that is just.

If the President can begin dismantling the unwise and unsuccessful social programs of the past, and begin diminishing the size, role and responsibility of the Federal Government in our national life, he will reverse a tide that has been running strong for forty years. Conceivably, he has settled upon an issue on which the long-awaited, long-predicted political realignment may come about.

The opposition in Congress, however, is not without resources. Several years ago, the incantatory term "defense" was the password to open the public purse. The politician who voted against "defense," whether used to describe a necessary weapons system or a superfluous base in the boondocks, did so at his political peril. In recent times, however, the vested interests of social spending have mastered the game, and woe betide the politician who votes "nay" on a bill labeled "health" or "education" or "anti-poverty."

More and more, however, these terms are being used to cover raids upon the public treasury; the hope is that the American people, or a majority, have caught on to the game.

But the President's commitment to jettison the failed programs of the past entails a determination to search out new and more hopeful avenues of progress. The President's call is not the bugle of retreat, but a signal to re-group and to come at the nation's social ills from a more productive direction. The President's belief is that the new direction requires the distribution of power away from the central government and back toward the states and cities and communities of the nation—back, specifically, to the people. And the President so asserted in his Second Inaugural:

> "...at home the shift from old policies to new will not be a retreat from our responsibilities, but a better way to progress.

> "Abroad and at home, the key to those new responsibilities lies in the placing and the division of responsibility. We have lived too long with the consequences of attempting to gather all power and responsibility in Washington."

There were other objectives on the Presidential agenda, as the final returns came in from California on November 7, 1972. High among them was the determination to impose executive discipline on the vast, stubborn and recalcitrant federal bureaucracy, to make it responsive to the nation's elected leadership, and less so to its own manifold vested interests. From Truman to Eisenhower to Kennedy, Presidents had despaired of making the bureaucracy respond to the will of the people, as expressed in the polling booth. President Nixon's special problem was that, as a Republican, he confronted not only the inherent inertia of every mass bureaucracy, but also the inherent political hostility of a bureaucracy built in the Democratic New Deal and battened on the Democratic Great Society.

One method of bypassing the bureaucracy already put in place in his first term was "revenue sharing"—a reform that had been the dream of progressive Democrats and Republicans for years. Through it, money was conveyed through the national bureaucracy to state and local governments—where the problems are, and the needs exist. This historic reform was generally conceded among the President's first-term legislative triumphs.

Immediately following re-election, the President adopted two more critical reforms. First, administrators of proven ability and loyalty from the White House Staff moved into high level positions in the major departments. The likelihood was strong that such men would impose the will of the White House on the bureaucracy, and not become ambassadors to the White House for the special interests of their departments. Secondly, several Cabinet officers were named Counsellors to the President, to bring these domestic affairs executives into daily and direct contact with the President and his staff. Through administrative changes such as these, the President hopes to make domestic policy in his second term more directly responsive to the majority of the American people. Certainly, if government is to retain the confidence and support of its citizens, it must respond to those citizens' desires and demands—as expressed at election time.

A government bureaucracy that moves, despite explicit public demand, against the public must soon find itself with an angry and alienated electorate. By 1972 that was not an inaccurate description of the situation in the United States.

Looking beyond his four years in office, the President saw another need of his nation, his party, his philosophy: The expansion of existing institutions and the creation of new institutions to articulate and defend the values and political beliefs that motivate the Republican Party, the building of new cadres of leadership to implement his own social and political philosophy, not just for the next four years, but over the next two decades.

As written earlier, liberals are not merely the dominant force within the Democratic Party, as are conservatives within the Republican Party. The former man the heights of Academia; they publish most of the nation's books; they dominate the national media; and, with rare exceptions, they control the big foundations and the public policy institutes dependent upon them.

If the President's political majority is to be an enduring entity, it must develop the institutions and train the individuals who will articulate its values and beliefs, and carry on its traditions. Republicans and conservatives have shown themselves capable of defeating liberals within the caucuses and conventions of their party, and on election day. They have yet to begin the serious building of a competing structure, an alternative establishment.

Where, for example, is the conservative or Republican alternative to the prestigious Brookings Institute in Washington, D.C., a tax-exempt public policy center that serves as a soldier's home for retired officers of the New Frontier and Great Society, and government-in-exile awaiting the restoration to power of the Democratic Party? Where are the socially active and politically aware foundations whose generosity, wealth and power can match the big foundations of political liberals?

Republicans and conservatives would do well in coming years to call public attention to this imbalancing feature in American politics, and to devise, create and support institutions to defend and advance the ideas and values of Middle America.

But, as 1973 opened, there were other great goals upon which all Americans agreed as to ends, but not as to means. Among these were alleviation of the environmental crisis and the energy crisis. In some respects, the two goals are in conflict. The environmentalists might argue that new power plants will further damage the nation's environment; those concerned with the energy shortage will argue that new power plants are not only necessary to the economic health of the nation, but essential, if the fouled environment is to be cleaned. The nature of the conflict is encapsulated in the half-jesting remark of the irrepressible Secretary of Agriculture, Earl Butz, who suggested that when the fuel oil shortages came, the first to be cut off should be the environmentalists who had opposed the building of the Alaska pipeline.

However, just as the President in his first term had raised the environment to the level of an issue of primary national importance, and created new government institutions to deal with that situation —so, in the opening days of the second term, "energy" seems to be emerging as such a crisis, with an equal claim upon the nation and the government's attention and concern.

Another issue dividing the nation in early 1973 was the clash between the President and Congress. Though liberals and intellectuals had been the foremost acolytes of executive power since the New Deal, by 1973 they had become the new champions of Congressional power.

Men who had bemoaned JFK's frustration and inability to enact legislation and who had applauded LBJ's mastery of Capitol Hill, were unenthusiastic when a Republican President—despite opposition control of both Houses—was showing himself as strong a President as the nation had ever known.

The latest struggle is another chapter in the never-ending conflict between the executive and the legislature for political power. But it guarantees that, whatever else occurs, the next four years will find the nation living in what the Chinese characterize as "interesting times."

What seems hopeful, as the final four years of the Nixon Presidency begin, is that the debate, the division, the conflicts, can take place not during years of war, but in a time of peace. There is no reason, at the outset of 1973, that the collision of evenly matched political forces cannot be of benefit to the entire nation.

In any event, regardless of the outcome—with the submission of the 1974 budget to Congress—the President has made clear his priorities, and the battle seems about to be joined.